# Animal Habitats

Previously published as six individual volumes:
*24 HOURS Coral Reef, Rain Forest, Water Hole,
Desert, Mountain,* and *Arctic.*

LONDON, NEW YORK, MUNICH,
MELBOURNE, and DELHI

**Editors** Caroline Bingham, Fleur Star,
Zahavit Shalev, Elizabeth Haldane,
Lorrie Mack
**Editor, this edition** Lorrie Mack

**Designers** Cathy Chesson, Jacqueline
Gooden, Tory Gordon-Harris, Mary
Sandberg, Karen Hood, Clare Shedden
**Designer, this edition** Hedi Hunter

**Consultants** Dr. Frances Dipper, Kerstin
Swahn, Julio Bernal, Evan Bowen-Jones,
Ginger Mauney, Berny Sèbe, Bryan and
Cherry Alexander
**Consultant, this edition** Kim
Dennis-Bryan PhD. FZS

**US editor** Margaret Parrish
**Production editor** Siu Chan
**Production controller** Claire Pearson
**Jacket designer** Natalie Godwin
**Jacket editor** Mariza O'Keeffe

**Publishing manager** Bridget Giles
**Art director** Rachael Foster
**Creative director** Jane Bull
**Publisher** Mary Ling

First published in the United States in 2009 by
DK Publishing
375 Hudson Street, New York, New York 10014

Copyright © 2009 Dorling Kindersley Limited

176802—07/09

A catalog record for this book
is available from the Library of Congress.

ISBN: 978-0-7566-5817-5

Color reproduction by Colourscan, Singapore,
and ICON, UK
Printed and bound in China by Toppan

Discover more at
**www.dk.com**

# Contents

# Introduction

In every corner of the Earth, millions of enchanting creatures are going about their business every second of every day. In the first light of dawn, for example, fennec foxes are snuggling down to sleep in the desert, while colorful triggerfish are coming out from a crack in the coral reef to search for delicious crabs and snails to eat.

### Key to habitats around the world

- Tropical forest and rain forest
- Temperate forest, including woodland
- Coniferous forest, including woodland
- Mountains, highlands, rocky slopes
- Desert and semidesert
- Open habitats including grassland, moorland, heathland, savanna, fields, scrub
- Coral reefs and waters immediately around them
- Polar regions, including tundra and icebergs

The Arctic

NORTH AMERICA

Tropic of Cancer

Equator

Pacific Ocean

SOUTH AMERICA

Tropic of Capricorn

In each of six chapters (Coral Reef, Rain Forest, Water Hole, Desert, Mountain, and Arctic), you can follow five specific animals as they go through a day and a night, and learn lots of fascinating facts about all the other creatures that share their habitat. Then, as you go through your day—having breakfast, going to school, playing with your friends, eating supper, getting ready for bed—you'll know exactly what all your favorite animals are doing at the same time!

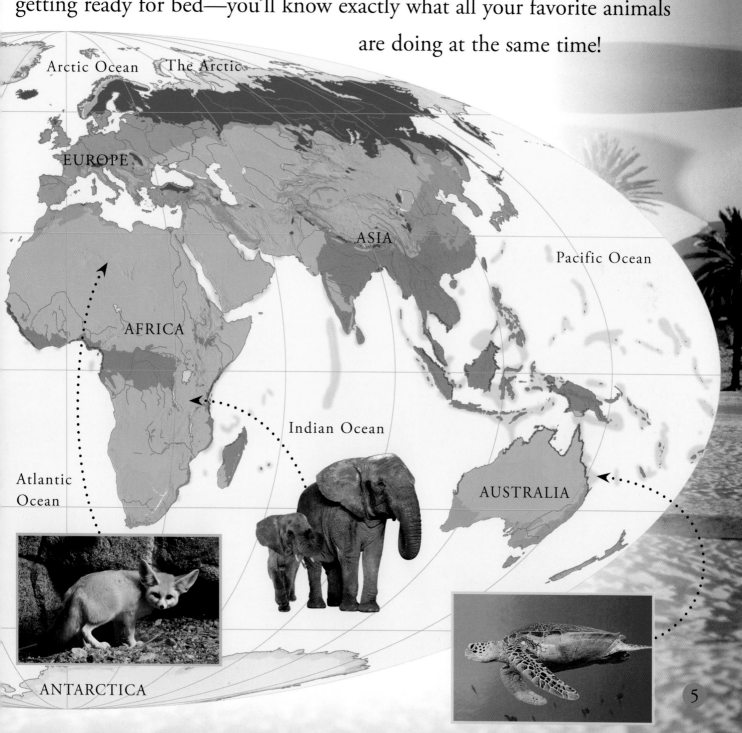

Arctic Ocean    The Arctic

EUROPE

ASIA

Pacific Ocean

AFRICA

Indian Ocean

Atlantic
Ocean

AUSTRALIA

ANTARCTICA

# Coral Reef

# Although they cover less than one percent of the Earth's surface, coral reefs are home to more than 15 percent of all fish species. Welcome to the coral reefs—the fabulous rain forests of the sea.

1 Moray eel   2 Butterflyfish   3 Turtle
4 Soft coral   5 Hard coral

**D**awn has broken over the "rainforest of the sea," the coral reef. Morning is a busy time on the reef as the fish wake up and begin their search for breakfast.

The **moray eel** is resting in his hole. He constantly opens and shuts his mouth, sucking fresh water over his gills to breathe.

The **turtle** is tired and hungry. She has had a busy night, laying more than 100 eggs on the beach. She's heading for the reef for breakfast.

The **triggerfish** has just woken up and emerged from his crevice. He is ready to go off hunting for crunchy crabs and sea snails.

The **bubble coral** senses it's morning because of the change in light. It has begun to expand its bubbles, or vesicles.

The **reef shark** has had a successful night's hunting. With a full tummy, she's now ready for a rest. She's a big fish, and smaller fish stay clear.

# Millions of tiny animals are visible to predators in bright light. During the day, they move down to the darker depths of the sea, because they don't want to be eaten. These are the zooplankton.

Some zooplankton look like miniatures of the adults they will become, like this shrimp larva.

Don't worry! This planktonic lobster larva is magnified thousands of times.

**The bottom of the ladder**
Plankton may be small, but without them, the corals and other sea life would not exist. They form the base of the sea's food chain.

"Plankton" comes from a Greek word that means "drifting."

**Rising to the surface**

There are two main types of plankton: phytoplankton and zooplankton. The first are tiny algae cells. Zooplankton are animals – many come up to the sea's surface at night to eat the phytoplankton.

Some plankton have spikes.

Phytoplankton use sunlight to produce much of the oxygen we breathe.

**In close-up**

Many plankton are so tiny that they can only be seen properly through a microscope. A drop of sea water may hold 100,000 phytoplankton.

**The daytime fish** are now very active. They tend to move higher above the coral as the light increases, but are quick to dart back to the safety of holes and crevices in the coral if danger threatens.

There are two main types of corals: hard and soft. **Hard corals** are the reef-building corals and have a protective stony base. Most feed at night. Many **soft corals** feed during the day and sway with the movement of the water. They contribute to the daytime colors of the reef.

A finger-sized squirt can filter a quart (liter) of sea water each hour.

**Suck, squirt**

Sea squirts show little reaction to changes of light. Day and night, they suck water in through one tube and squirt it out of another.

Soft corals tend to grow on overhangs and cliffs.

**Batfish** often swim behind turtles, vacuuming up the scraps of food the turtles drop. Black stripes across their eyes help to disguise the vulnerable head: the aim is for the predator to attack the tail, so that the batfish can escape.

There are more than 100 different types of butterflyfish. All have beautiful markings.

Like many reef fish, **butterflyfish** have flattened bodies, perfect for nipping in between the corals. Butterflyfish indicate the health of a reef. The greater the number and variety, the healthier the reef. Butterflyfish often swim in pairs.

It's difficult to see, but a fierce battle is taking place on the reef. **Corals** are always competing for space and light, as are simple reef animals called **sponges**. It can be a battle to the death when one grows over the other.

Corals are animals. Hard corals settle on the sea floor and on slopes.

13

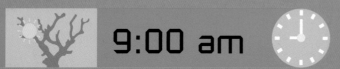
**Some fish** don't need to hide, even in the bright light of morning. In fact, many fish have odd but effective ways of making sure they don't become a bigger fish's snack. Some have poisonous stingers, while others are just so well camouflaged that they are very difficult to spot.

Parrotfish take their name from their bright colors, their flapping fins, and their beaks.

### From fish to beach

Parrotfish grind down the rocky coral they eat and pass it out as sand. It's amazing, but true, that in this way just one parrotfish creates many pounds (kilograms) of sand each year— sand that finds its way to tropical beaches.

Parrotfish are .....
grazers, and scrape algae off corals. Bumpheads eat the coral, too.

### Bony beak

A parrotfish's beak is made of fused teeth. It is an ideal tool for chiseling away at the reef. Parrotfish are sometimes called the "cows of the sea."

**Midday** and the burning sun is overhead. The promise of a lazy afternoon washes over the reef. The morning rush is over, and there's plenty of time to look at a few of the giants of the reef: the curiously shaped sponges, the giant manta ray, and the amazing giant clam.

The **barrel sponge** may look like a plant, but sponges are simple animals. Sponges are covered in tiny holes through which they draw in water, taking out the food and oxygen they need. Barrel sponges can grow to reach 3 ft (1 m) in height.

Established sponges cannot move, unlike most animals. They feed on tiny particles of food in the water.

Mouth

With a lazy flap of its winglike fins, a **giant manta ray** glides slowly by. From wingtip to wingtip, these creatures can be as wide as a small airplane.

Manta rays are filter-feeders, scooping in plankton-rich sea water. These gentle giants can live for about 20 years.

It's 3 feet (1 m) across and very heavy.

Many people see mollusks every day in the form of slugs and snails. The **giant clam** is also a mollusk. By midday, the clam's shell is wide open, exposing its fleshy lips to the sunlight.

21

**It's early** afternoon and time for a wash and brush at the local cleaning station.

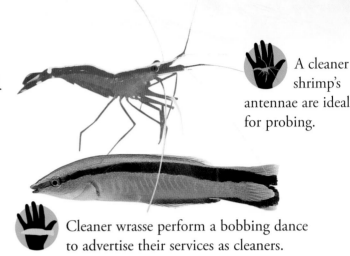

A cleaner shrimp's antennae are ideal for probing.

Cleaner wrasse perform a bobbing dance to advertise their services as cleaners.

Cleaning stations do big business on the daytime reef. It's a place where fish and turtles go to get cleaned up.

Table coral provides a good platform for a cleaning station's line.

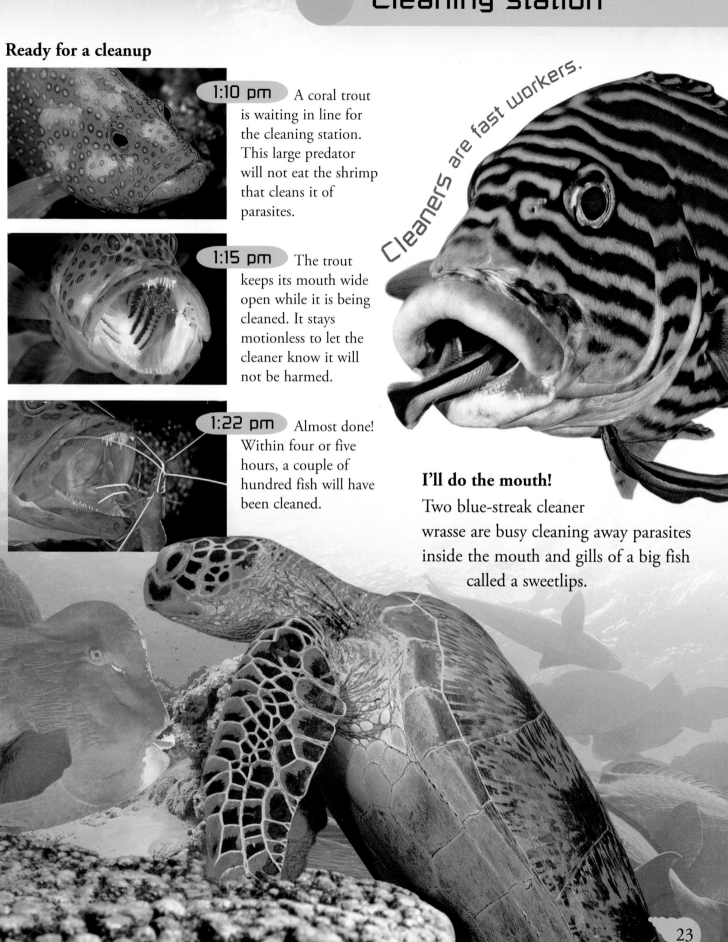

## Ready for a cleanup

**1:10 pm** A coral trout is waiting in line for the cleaning station. This large predator will not eat the shrimp that cleans it of parasites.

**1:15 pm** The trout keeps its mouth wide open while it is being cleaned. It stays motionless to let the cleaner know it will not be harmed.

**1:22 pm** Almost done! Within four or five hours, a couple of hundred fish will have been cleaned.

_Cleaners are fast workers._

### I'll do the mouth!

Two blue-streak cleaner wrasse are busy cleaning away parasites inside the mouth and gills of a big fish called a sweetlips.

**1** Turtle  **2** Sea fir  **3** Manta ray

By 2 pm the reef is a little quieter. The daytime animals have had their breakfast and lunch, and the nighttime animals are still resting. Small fish ignore the passing manta ray, still busy scooping up plankton.

The **moray eel** is taking his turn at the cleaning station. Morays are messy eaters, and they need frequent cleaning.

The **turtle** is nibbling sea grass. Adult green turtles spend lots of their time eating sea grass, mangrove roots, and leaves.

The **triggerfish** is tending to his eggs, and is keeping them clean by blowing sand away. He also blows sand to uncover hidden animals.

A close look at the **bubble coral** reveals tiny creatures living safely among its bubbles— like this little shrimp.

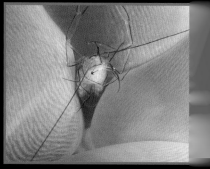

The **reef shark** has found a deep crevice in which to hide. She's still resting—she won't be very active until the sun goes down.

Anemone-
fish

It's **midafternoon** and an anemonefish is hovering above its protective host, a sea anemone. The anemone's tentacles are loaded with **stinging** cells whose **venom** is enough to keep most **fish away**—but not anemonefish, which have a **protective** coat of slime.

Some sea anemones close up into a tight ball if threatened.

The winking lights are used to signal other flashlight fish and to confuse predators.

Some fish, such as these **flashlight fish,** can make their own light with the help of bacteria. Flashlight fish live deep down, but rise higher on moonless nights. They can switch off their light by covering it with a skin flap.

## Appearance of a Christmas tree

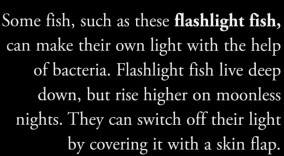

Before This worm has been startled, probably by the photographer, and has withdrawn.

After The worm senses that any danger has gone, and slowly unfolds its pretty tentacles once more.

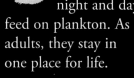

**Christmas tree worms emerge** night and day to feed on plankton. As adults, they stay in one place for life.

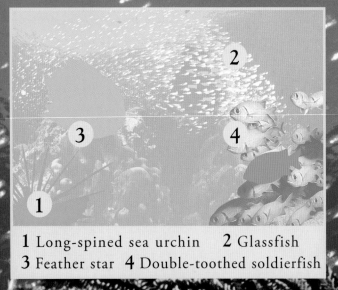

1 Long-spined sea urchin   2 Glassfish
3 Feather star  4 Double-toothed soldierfish

**I**t is late and the nighttime fish have taken over the reef. Tiny glassfish create a flash of shimmering silver, while a small shoal of soldierfish feast on the plankton that have risen higher in the water.

The **moray eel** has seized his chance and ambushed an unwary fish. Once he has it in his jaws, he will swallow it whole.

The **turtle** has been sleeping on a ledge. She now needs to swim up and take a few gasps of air. Then she will settle down again.

The **triggerfish** is near his crevice. For extra safety, he can wedge himself in by locking his "trigger," a strong spine in his dorsal fin.

During the night, the **bubble coral** sometimes withdraws all its tentacles, as well as its bubbles, revealing its hard skeleton.

The **reef shark** has been joined by others. They will swim over the reef during the night, hunting for fish, and will strike with lightning speed.

It is now deep into the night and sharks are swimming back and forth over the reef, hunting for food. One of the strangest-looking sharks of all is the hammerhead.

The largest hammerheads grow to more than 13 ft (4-m) in length.

**Why a "hammerhead"?**
It is thought that the hammerhead's unusual head shape helps this shark sense its prey's position in the water. Sharks do this by picking up small electrical signals that the victim sends out as it moves.

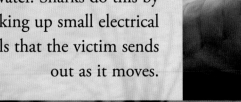

...breakthrough!

**I'll come out now!**
Baby turtles use a special egg tooth to
break out of their soft, leathery egg shell.
They can then take a couple of days to
dig out of their sandy nest.

The babies head for the sea as fast as they can.

Artificial light can
make some babies
head the wrong way. They
are under immediate threat
from ghost crabs, seabirds,
and lizards.

# Rain Forest

As busy as a city, the amazing Amazon rain forest houses millions of colorful creatures that do lots of the same things we do, like sleep, and eat, and play. Come and explore the biggest jungle in the world!

An emergent tree breaks through the rain-forest canopy.

**Dawn** is a swift affair in the Amazon, so close to the equator. Sunrise is at the same time all year. As soon as the sun climbs above the canopy, it begins to filter through the trees to warm the forest.

The **jaguar** is settling down to sleep after a successful night's hunting. On lean days, jaguars will continue to hunt through the day.

The **capuchin monkey** is just beginning its day. It moves from its sleeping tree to an eating tree, where it peels the bark, looking for insects.

**Scarlet macaws** (on left) flock together at the clay lick before breakfast. Eating clay protects them against toxins in the seeds they eat.

The **blue morpho** is pupating—changing from a caterpillar to a butterfly. Its chrysalis has been hanging off of a leaf for a few weeks now.

Hummingbirds are ideal pollinators of **heliconia** flowers. Attracted by the plant's bright red bracts, the birds are rewarded with plenty of nectar.

# Howler monkeys are noisy beasts! Having woken the rain forest at dawn with their loud roars, which can be heard **10 miles** (16 km) away, they go foraging for breakfast.

Howlers can **hang** upside-down to feast on fruit and **leaves**.

Howler monkeys are territorial—they "howl" to keep other monkeys out.

A baby hangs on to its mother's fur. It is too young to forage for itself.

# The dawn chorus

Both red howler and black howler species live in the Amazon rain forest.

Howwlll

### Call of nature
The dawn chorus starts with a single male howler's call, which sounds like a breathless bark. Other howlers join in, and the howls grow louder and longer until a roar fills the forest.

# Once the macaws
have lined their stomachs with clay, they may fly to a Brazil nut tree for a nutty breakfast. Howler monkeys, sloths, and caterpillars can also be found in the tree's canopy, munching on the juicy green leaves.

No animal could eat Brazil nuts if it weren't for the **agouti**. It is the only creature that can break through the tough outer pod, releasing the nuts inside.

**Living for** up to 1,000 years, Brazil-nut trees are the oldest in the forest. They are also among the tallest, and can even change the local weather! Together they release enough water from their leaves to form rain clouds.

"I'll **nibble** a few nuts now, and bury the rest for later."

The agouti chisels through the pod with its sharp rodent teeth.

54

Brazil nuts are clustered inside a pod as heavy as a cannonball.

Capuchins drink the nuts' oil as well as eating the kernels.

**Bright blue bees** are the key to the Brazil nut's success. They are the only insect that can pollinate the tree—and if there is no pollination, there are no seeds and no new trees.

These bees are called orchid bees because they use the scent of orchids to attract mates.

A buzz of activity surrounds a fig tree, with many different animals turning up to feed on figs. The trees produce fruit all year, even during the dry season when other trees are bare.

### The cycle of life

**9:15 am** Figs can only be pollinated by tiny fig wasps. The female crawls inside through a tiny hole, carrying pollen with her.

Up to 20 species of fig trees can grow together in the same area of forest, each with its own shape and size of fruit. The largest is the size of a tennis ball.

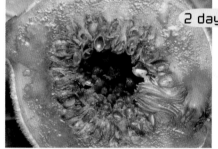

**2 days later** She lays her eggs inside the fig, pollinating the flowers at the same time. Fig wasps can only reproduce inside figs.

**30 days later** The young wasps leave home and fly to another fig to lay their own eggs, taking pollen with them, and the cycle begins again.

A fig is made up of lots of flowers growing inside a skin...

Figs can only ripen if they have been pollinated. The wasps leave the fruit before it ripens.

# Figs for all

## More animals eat figs than any other fruit...

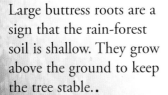

Vines and lianas grow on most trees in the rain forest, weighing them down and competing for light and nutrients.

Large buttress roots are a sign that the rain-forest soil is shallow. They grow above the ground to keep the tree stable..

 **Butterflies** feast on figs on the forest floor. A butterfly cannot chew; instead, it sucks up fruit pulp through its tube-shaped mouth, called a proboscis.

Safe in its roost, a **tent-building bat** eats a fig fresh from the tree. It carefully peels away the unripe skin with its teeth before eating the seeds inside.

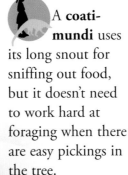 A **coati-mundi** uses its long snout for sniffing out food, but it doesn't need to work hard at foraging when there are easy pickings in the tree.

The strong bill of a **blue and yellow macaw** rips through fig skin easily. Macaws are the only birds that can pick up food in their claws to bring it to their mouths.

**10:00 am**

1 Jaguar   2 Spider monkey

**M**idmorning, the sun streams through the trees and heats the forest to 80°F (27°C). An alert jaguar finds a shady spot on the forest floor. It would usually be asleep during the day, but hunger drives it to hunt.

Up in a tree, the **jaguar's** spotted fur looks like sunlight shining through the leaves. It has no tree-climbing predators and can sleep safely up there.

Apart from a nap at noon, **capuchins** spend much of the day eating. They are very intelligent and use tools such as stones to crack nutshells.

A **macaw's** strong bill is not just a mouth, it is an extra limb. As well as crushing food, the macaw's bill can grip branches while climbing.

The **blue morpho** chrysalis splits and, after 20 minutes, the imago—adult butterfly—emerges. It then rests for two hours to dry its wings.

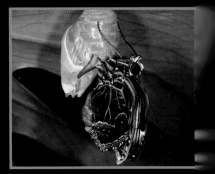

Tent-building bats use large **heliconia** leaves as a daytime roost. They chew the leaves to make them droop, giving shelter from rain, sun, and predators.

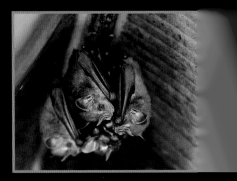

A smash-and-grab raid is taking place in broad daylight. A giant anteater has sniffed out a termite mound, and sits down to dig its snout into a meal. Its long, thin tongue dips in and out of the nest 160 times a minute, scooping up the insects.

**Anteaters' long snouts** are not just straws for sucking up food; they also use their noses to find ants' nests and termite mounds. They have poor eyesight, so they rely on their sense of smell. If the insects are hard to reach, anteaters will rip the nests apart with their powerful claws.

### Azteca ants fight back

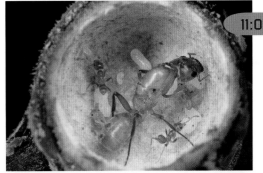

**11:00 am** Azteca ants, a favorite of tamandua anteaters, live inside cecropia tree branches. The tree even provides food for the ants.

**1 day later** Without damaging the tree, the queen ant lays her eggs inside a narrow stem. It is a home safe from predators.

**8 days later** In return, the ants attack animals that eat the tree. They can also see off tamanduas with a flurry of bites.

**Leafcutter ants** stream along the forest floor in a parade of nibbled leaves, carrying them back to their nest.

The ants feed on fungus, which grows on the chewed leaves.

Every rain forest around the world is home to primates, from Asian orangutans to Madagascan lemurs. South America seems to specialize in small monkeys that enjoy playing in the sun!

Tree-dwelling tamarins eat whatever they can find in the canopy, from eggs to fruit.

Spider monkeys have small or no thumbs on their hands: swinging through trees is easier with just four fingers.

Squirrel-sized **tamarins** get around by leaping between trees. They can jump 65 ft (20 m) to the ground and land unhurt.

All **silvery marmosets** are born as twins. They feed on sap straight from the tree.

Spider monkeys are the rain-forest acrobats, active all day and using their tails for climbing. But they do not climb too high in the canopy, to avoid becoming a harpy eagle's lunch.

The **jaguar** has found shelter in dense brush to avoid the rain. A short shower barely reaches the forest floor through the closely growing trees.

The sociable **capuchins** have stopped their daytime grooming and foraging to shelter from the rain. They huddle together for warmth.

**Macaws** should be out finding food for their chicks, but the rain forces them to stay in their nest. Many chicks starve during heavy rains.

Having dried its wings, which are now bright and shimmering, the **blue morpho** flies down to the forest floor to eat its first meal as an adult.

Rainwater collects in the **heliconia's** bracts, where insects such as mosquitoes lay their eggs. Bigger animals will also drink the water.

# The rain has stopped, the heat returns, and the animals reappear. Or do they? Some of them are hard to spot. Insects use camouflage to hide from predators, but iguanas blend in with trees so they can catch insects undetected.

**Iguanas** also stay hidden to avoid predators. If spotted, they will drop off the branches to escape being caught. Iguanas can fall more than 60 ft (18 m) without being hurt.

The fixed pose of a **praying mantis** can easily be mistaken for a twig.

The underside of a **blue morpho's** wings is not blue, but brown— the perfect camouflage for the forest floor.

Some insects have weird disguises to stay hidden in the daytime.

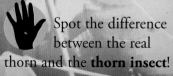

Spot the difference between the real thorn and the **thorn insect**!

Katydids are masters of disguise. A **dead-leaf katydid** becomes part of the forest floor...

Is this an owl or an **owl butterfly**? The insect has "eye spots" on its wings to confuse and scare off predators such as pacas, which are targets for owls.

...while up in the tree, a **green-leaf katydid** is just one of the crowd.

*Eek!*

Lichen grows on some tree trunks. It is a safe home for the spiky **lichen katydid**.

A **conehead katydid's** spines are used for defense, but they also help the insect hide among thorns.

# Far from hiding in the understory

like insects, birds are a noticeable part of the rain forest. Males are free to show off their bright colors to attract females; at the first sign of a predator, they quickly fly away.

A **toucan** reaches out with its bill to pluck fruit. Its bill is so long, it has to toss its head back and throw the fig into its throat to swallow it.

The **cock of the rock** lives in mountainous parts of the forest. It is vital to the forests because it disperses the seeds of many trees.

The **scarlet tanager** is one of the few rain-forest birds that migrates, spending the summer in North America.

The manakin's courtship dance includes raising its tail and cracking it like a whip.

Two male **manakins** put on a display in their lek, an area where birds show off to attract mates.

Of the 27 species of parrots in the rain forest, the **hyacinth macaw** stands head and shoulders above the rest, being 3 ft (1 m) long from head to tail. These macaws are usually seen in the trees, only coming to the ground for food.

Many tank bromeliads grow on trees, using them to get near the sunlight. Other bromeliads live on the ground.

Bromeliads are ideal daytime hideouts for nocturnal frogs. Tiny **red-eyed tree frogs** can rest inside the leaves safe from predators.

In among the trees are thousands of tank bromeliads. They provide a watery home for small animals, and a drinking fountain for larger ones.

Pineapples are bromeliads, but they do not have tanks. The spiky leaves are the beginnings of a new plant.

72

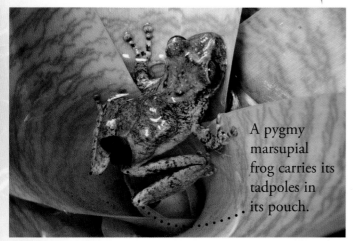

A pygmy marsupial frog carries its tadpoles in its pouch.

## Birthing pool

Tadpoles live in water, so most frogs in the Amazon rainforest lay their eggs in bromeliad pools, but some lay on the forest floor. The mother then gives the tadpoles a piggyback ride up to the water.

Bromeliad leaves are stiff and strong, easily taking the weight of a passing **lizard** that has come to drink the water. The nutrients in the water also feed the plant.

Some species of tank bromeliads can hold 12 gallons (45 liters) of water!

The plant's leaves grow in a spiral, with the flowers in the middle. Most only flower once, then die.

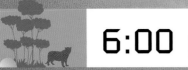

Rain-forest clouds turn the setting sun's rays into a haze.

**T**he sun sets quickly in the rain forest. There is little time for dusky half-light; as the sun dips behind the canopy, the forest falls dark. It also fills with the sound of frogs, bats, and insects as sunset brings them out for the night.

# Going batty

**A sac-winged bat** is among the first to leave its daytime roost as the sun sets. The insect-hunter lives in groups of up to 50 bats that roost on the buttress roots of trees.

The bones that stretch out the wing are the bat's fingers. The wing itself is made of skin.

## How to go fishing without a net

**8:29 pm**  A low-flying fishing bat searches the river for minnows. Its echolocation works through the water.

**8:30 pm**  In the blink of an eye, the bat swoops in on its prey and scoops up the unsuspecting fish in its claws.

*they can hear insects without using echolocation.*

**Carnivorous bats** track their prey using echolocation. They send out a click and listen for the echo to return. If it returns quickly, that means something is nearby.

Leaf-nosed bats click through their large, pointed noses. The clicks are louder than those made by bats that use their mouths.

# Sloths sleep for 15 hours a day, yet they are barely more active when awake. They move most at night, when they are less visible to predators.

A baby sloth hitches a ride on its mother's stomach until it is strong enough to hang from branches. . . . . . . . .

**Going green**
Algae grows in the sloth's long fur, especially in the rainy season. It provides useful camouflage for the slow-moving animal.

Sloths eat only leaves, which don't provide much energy.

## Just hanging around

With their long legs and hooked claws, sloths are built for life in the trees. Their front legs are so long that they cannot walk properly on the ground.

Sloths look like they are grinning all the time. To save energy, they don't ever change their expression.

## Coming down to earth

**9:10 pm** About every eight days, the sloth inches down the tree to the ground to go to the bathroom.

**9:30 pm** Once on the ground, the sloth defecates at the base of the tree. The dung is good fertilizer for the tree.

**9:35 pm** Sloth moths live in the sloth's fur, leaving it only to lay their eggs and feed on the dung.

1 Paca  2 Common lancehead snake

A startled paca stops in its tracks as it spots a camouflaged snake while out foraging. The highly poisonous common lancehead detects prey through the heat the animal gives out, and strikes with extreme speed.

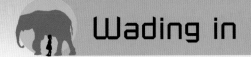 

## Elephant skincare

If these elephants look a little dusty, that's because they are! After bathing, elephants suck dust into their trunks and then dump it all over their bodies. It acts as an insect repellent, and stops the sun from damaging their skin.

## Bathtime for a baby elephant

**10:02 am** This baby elephant is feeling a bit uncertain about getting into the water and dithers hesitantly at the water's edge...

**10:03 am** A caring, motherly trunk reaches out. It first coaxes, and then gently pushes, the little elephant in.

**10:25 am** Once in the water, all fears are forgotten. Adults and baby play contentedly in the cool water.

...but these springboks **scramble** out of the **way** when they approach!

Elephants are very steady because they always have three feet on the the ground....

95

**The area surrounding** the water hole is patterned with paths the elephants have created as they travel between the water hole and the forested areas where they go to eat leaves.

Insects and other creatures disturbed by the elephants' heavy tread are swiftly snapped up by waiting birds.

Elephants walk at a leisurely 3 miles (5 km) per hour, but they

**Elephants can communicate** with each other over distances as far as 1½ miles (2.5 km). We can't hear these sounds, so it surprises us when many elephants suddenly arrive at the water hole at the same time.

can **run** at 25 miles (40 km)

### Recycling elephant dung

**8:10 am** Since it doesn't digest its food fully, a lot of useful matter remains in the 220 pounds (100 kg) of dung produced by an **elephant** each day.

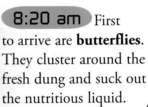

**8:20 am** First to arrive are **butterflies**. They cluster around the fresh dung and suck out the nutritious liquid.

**10:00 am** **Birds** eat the seeds contained in the dung, and pluck out undigested grass and straw to use in building their nests.

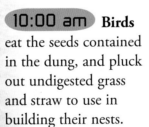

**5:00 pm** **Dung beetles** form the dung into small, compact balls. They determinedly roll these to their tunnels and lay eggs on them.

**11:00 pm** If what remains by now is damp enough, **mushrooms** may start to sprout from the dung pile. That means food for yet more animals.

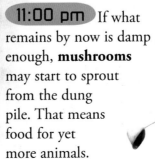

97

# There's safety in numbers for the members of a herd. If you're a strong healthy animal and a hungry lion appears while you're grazing, there's a good chance the unlucky victim will be someone else!

**Most grazing animals** drink at least once every day, so they can't stray far from the water hole. The tracks they make as they travel between feeding grounds and the water hole are etched into the landscape.

When food is scarce, impalas have less energy, and so are more vulnerable to predators.

*If attacked, this tranquil herd of impalas will* **explode** *into a chaotic frenzy of leaping to* **confuse** *their attackers.*

Spotted hyenas sometimes hunt alone but usually do better by cooperating and hunting in packs.

*zebra or even a wildebeest.*

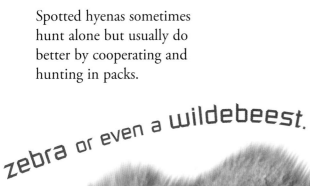

**Providing food for the family**

**10:29 am** Black-backed jackals will eat most things. A jackal attacks a flock of sand grouse by the water's edge, making them scatter.

**10:33 am** Having caught and killed a bird, this jackal has to avoid having its prize snatched away by bigger predators on the way home.

**10:40 am** Three hungry cubs are waiting for their share back at the den. In a few months, they, too, will be out hunting for food.

It's great being tall. Giraffes can reach the juicy leaves at the top of the tree and see hungry lions a long way off. But there's at least one big disadvantage—it's a long way down to get a drink.

**Responsible drinking**

11:02 am It's safe to drink, so this giraffe starts to move its front legs apart.

Giraffes roam in small herds of between three and 20 animals with no obvious leader.

This giraffe is taller than three tall men standing on each other's heads!

A giraffe has just **seven** bones in its neck, the **same** number as you.

## Looking out for danger

Bending over is tricky, and getting up is even harder. A thirsty giraffe can spend hours making sure it's absolutely safe before quenching its thirst.

**11:08 am** Long legs move out some more and then the head goes down.

**11:15 am** One-way valves in the giraffe's neck stop blood from suddenly flooding its brain.

**The birds** that visit the water hole are extremely varied. They range from enormous ostriches to tiny oxpeckers, flesh-eating storks to insect-crunching hornbills, and group-loving guineafowl to solitary storks.

Delicate and pretty they may be, but **lilac-breasted rollers** make a surprisingly harsh squawking sound!

Oxpeckers and giraffes form an **unlikely** partnership. The little birds keep the giraffes free of **ticks** and **fleas**.

**Oxpeckers** have been known to take advantage of their host by keeping the giraffe's insect wounds open so they can feed on its blood.

**Ostriches** are the largest birds in the world. They don't need much water but they travel far in search of food even though they are unable to fly.

Young baboons playfully chase one another up the branches of a tree, and scamper around the trunk.

During a friendly grooming session, the baboon doing the grooming gets to eat all the **juicy** bugs it finds!

### One of the gang

Being a baboon means doing everything together. Baboon gangs sleep in the same tree, and spend their days nearby looking for food, and drinking at the water hole.

During grooming, baboons lick each other. They love the salty taste.

111

The relatively few trees dotting the landscape have very deep roots that enable them to survive long periods with no rain. Their leaves and fruit provide food for a variety of insects, birds, and small animals.

Sociable weaver birds build enormous nests. Each bird has its own "apartment."

Black mambas can move as fast as you can run. And their venom is deadly.

# Tree for all

About 40 baboons sleep at this baboon base camp and spend the day on the ground nearby.

## Clever killers

**Boomslangs** climb trees and slither between branches to catch lizards and even birds. They strike at their prey, injecting it with poisonous venom.

**Skinks** scuttle around looking for spiders and insects to eat. If attacked, a skink can shed its tail in order to make a quick getaway.

This mother **scorpion** carries her babies on her back. Over time, their exoskeletons (bony coverings) will gradually darken and harden.

Unusually for an owl, the **pearl-spotted owlet** often hunts by day. Despite its small size, it is very strong and isn't afraid to attack prey bigger than itself.

**Combretum trees** can grow very large. Rhinos love to munch on the young leaves. As the tree grows older, deep cracks form in the bark, which will provide homes for many small creatures.

Warthogs normally live in burrows that have been dug by other animals.

**The dusty earth** looks uninviting, but many insects and reptiles find somewhere to live and a plentiful supply of food on or just below the ground. When the heat gets unbearable, they sit it out underground or in water and wait for cooler days.

Impressive tusks are used for defense against lions and leopards. The lower set is very sharp.

Two pairs of bumpy "warts" between eyes and tusks give this peculiar-looking animal its name.

Like their piggy cooling wallow

**Fresh meat for dinner**

**8:03 pm** After many hours in wait, a lioness selects her target—one of the weaker kudus in the herd.

**8:04 pm** She runs powerfully toward her victim. Panicking, the kudu notices too late and tries to flee.

**8:05 pm** The lioness grabs the kudu. With a swipe at the legs and a bite to the spine, this kudu stands no chance.

**8:15 pm** Other lions who joined in the hunt dig in for a big meal. The next few hours will be spent digesting!

# Yawnnnnn

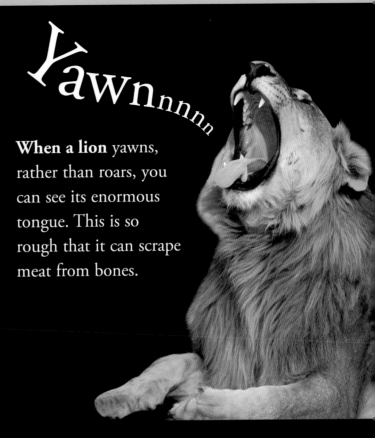

**When a lion** yawns, rather than roars, you can see its enormous tongue. This is so rough that it can scrape meat from bones.

Lion cubs in the lair greet their mother excitedly on her return from a hunting trip. She leads them to her kill for a share of the meat.

Lions prefer fresh meat, but the leftovers don't just lie around decomposing. Scavengers polish them off. They'll eat anything that was once alive! As nature's garbage collectors and recyclers, they consume every last scrap of flesh and bone left by the big hunters.

The lion in the pride hangs back. He watches distance and then barges

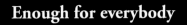

**Lionesses drink** after a kill. Although they are the hunters and actually do all the hard work, the males of the pride usually eat first, followed by the lionesses, and then the cubs.

the action lazily from a

in to get the first bite!

This wildebeest will be just a skeleton within a few hours. Only a very hungry hyena would devour the bones.

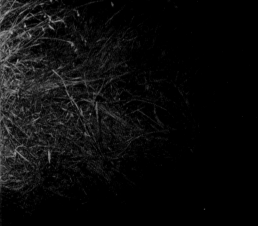

## Enough for everybody

**9:14 pm** High in the sky, **African white-backed vultures** use their amazing eyesight to spot the dead wildebeest far below. They make cackling and hissing sounds as they feast.

**9:21 pm** **Hyenas** arrive as the vultures leave. They bolt their food down, eating as much as a third of their own body weight, before trotting off across the plains.

**9:25 pm** **Lappet-faced vultures** scare the hyenas away. By ripping through the wildebeest's hide with their hooked beaks, they make it easier for other scavengers to feed next.

**9:46 pm** **Black-backed jackals** eat quickly, expecting to be pushed out of the way when larger scavengers arrive. Back in their den, they regurgitate some food for their young.

**9:50 pm** **Marabou storks** pick at the flesh of the wildebeest. They are bald so there are no feathers to get messy when they poke their heads into the rotting carcass.

**1** Rhinoceros   **2** Giraffe

Late at night the rustling of the undergrowth signals the arrival of rhinos and giraffes. Many other large animals, including elephants and lions, also come to drink during the cool hours of darkness.

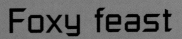

The foxes' diet includes moisture-rich plants, eggs, and birds such as the sandgrouse...

... And any animal small enough for them to catch. Lizards and desert locusts make a crunchy snack!

**Between a rock and a hard place**

Out in the open, the foxes face predators such as birds of prey. Their pale, sandy-colored fur provides some camouflage, but it is safer to hide inside a cave or in crevice among the rocks.

Small rodents, such as gerbils, are pounced on much like a cat catches mice.

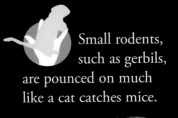

**Feeding the family**

Fennec fox cubs feed on their mother's milk until they are one month old. Once they are weaned, the male will stop bringing the female food and she leaves the den to hunt for herself.

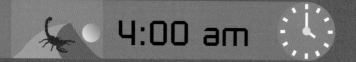 

# Scorpions are probably the oldest stinging things in existence. They stay hidden under rocks or in burrows during the day and come out at night to hunt—as does the fast-moving camel spider.

### Multiple birth

Scorpions give birth to up to 100 live young. The newborn scorpions climb up their mother's legs and onto her back. They stay there until their first molt a few days after their birth.

The babies get a ride until they can fend for themselves.

The yellow scorpion has the strongest venom of all scorpions and is very quick to sting. The pincers are used to hold prey.

The armadillo is only active in the daytime during winter. Summer heat forces it to turn its day around, searching for food at night and spending the day in cool burrows.

Armadillos live alone, only sharing burrows with their young. ....

The word "armadillo" means little plated one.

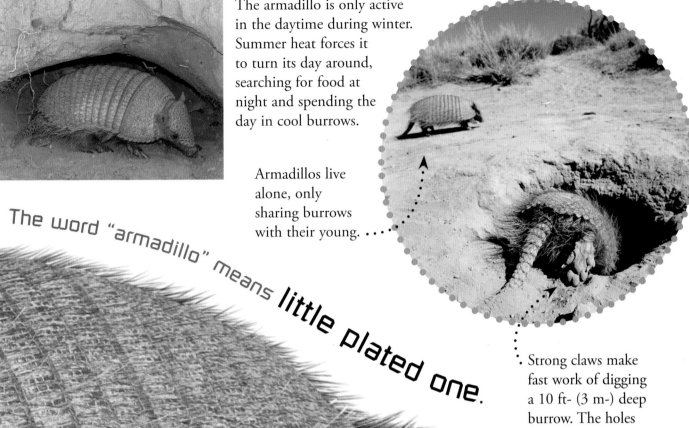

Strong claws make fast work of digging a 10 ft- (3 m-) deep burrow. The holes are only used once.

The best place to hide from predators is underground, but when there's no burrow to dive into the armadillo covers its legs and relies on its armor plating.

179

1 Juvenile Andean condor
2 Adult male Andean condor

J ust as there are high peaks in mountainous territory, there are also deep valleys. Colca Canyon is thought to be the world's deepest gorge (narrow valley). The steep slopes are a favored roosting site for Andean condors.

**First come, first served**

The birds gather around the day's meal in a strict pecking order. Males eat first; they are bigger than the females and perform displays to frighten off other scavengers that might be around. They rarely fight, because that could damage their feathers.

**Having gorged** itself on guanaco, this young **condor** waits for a thermal (air current) to carry it into flight. It has eaten too much to take off itself.

The flock COVERS the carcass.

On the dry grasslands, guanacos keep themselves clean not with water, but by rolling in a dust bath.

# Herds of grazing

guanacos are a familar sight across the Andean slopes, especially browsing plants on the puna grasslands. There are four species of South American camelid: guanacos and vicuñas are wild, but llamas and alpacas are farmed.

**Most herds are** family groups of one male leading lots of females and their young, which are called crias. Young males without mates form herds of their own; older males wander the mountains alone.

Guanacos chew their food by grinding it against their hard gums.

186

Teams of **neotropic cormorants** work together to get food. They wade through the lake, flapping their wings to chase the fish into shallow water.

The lake teems with **fish**, which **attract** lots of birds.

Argentine
silverside
fish

Killifish

The **puna ibis** uses its long, curved bill to probe for food in the shallow waters and the mud around the edge of the lake. Groups of ibis feed together, seeking fish, frogs, and small aquatic animals to eat.

**Three's a crowd**

Three species of flamingos live on the lakes: Andean, Chilean, and Puna. As soon as the birds arrive, they start the search for a mate.

**At the start** of the rainy season, flocks of flamingos settle on the **salt lakes** in the Altiplano. The lakes are far smaller than Lake Titicaca, yet **thousands** of birds feed here.

There's no competition between the three species as they eat different food.

Flamingos turn pink from the carotenoids in the algae or shrimp they eat. It's the same pigment that turns carrots orange.

Unlike guanacos, **vicuñas** drink lots of water during the day. They never stray far from rivers or lakes when grazing on the rocky slopes.

The **spectacled bear** leaves its tree to search the forest and paramo for food. Although mostly vegetarian, it will also eat small animals.

The **culpeo** rouses itself from its daytime rest to go hunting. A male culpeo with young cubs needs to get food for his family as well as himself.

Feeding and preening all day must be tiring work for an **Andean condor**! Giving a huge yawn, it prepares to return to its roost for the night.

From a high point on the peaks, the **puma** scans the mountains for prey. It prefers large deer or guanaco, but any meat will do.

With its thick fur, grooming is an important part of viscacha hair care! ...

Perched on a rock, a male viscacha watches for predators while his colony feeds. At the first sign of danger, he will call out a warning.

Viscachas have many predators,

**A young viscacha** stirs from sunbathing with a big stretch. It's time to find food, which young viscachas are able to eat as soon as they are born.

# Arctic fast food

Gyrfalcons need lemmings—when there are lots of lemmings, there are lots of gyrfalcons, too.

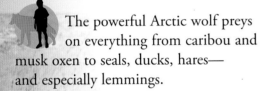

Snowy owls eat mostly lemmings, so when there aren't enough of them, snowy numbers drop dramatically.

Ermines may look sweet to us, but lemmings and voles—their chief prey—are terrified of them.

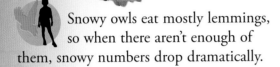

The powerful Arctic wolf preys on everything from caribou and musk oxen to seals, ducks, hares— and especially lemmings.

Small mammals in general—and lemmings in particular—make up the Arctic fox's diet.

Lemmings are a big favorite of the wolverine, but it will eat other small animals—and some very big ones, too!

# Mighty musk oxen are the only Arctic creatures who never need to seek shelter, no matter how **bitter** and **blizzardy** it gets. Their name comes from the strong **scent** the males develop during the mating season.

*This scary formation*

**Coat of many layers**

Each musk ox has a covering of coarse, shaggy hair (called guard hair) that hangs down like a long skirt over its stocky body. Underneath this are fine, soft hairs that provide lightweight insulation.

Arctic deer (like this caribou) use their hooves and snouts to get at grasses and lichens under the crusty snow.

Both caribou and reindeer migrate huge distances (up to 600 miles/1,000 km), but reindeer like these are usually accompanied by native human herders.

An Arctic deer's hooves help it to paddle in water and walk on snow. These caribou are crossing a river on the route of their fall migration.

241

### Survival of the fiercest

Jaegers are large, aggressive seabirds that eat small mammals, fish, and other birds. This one is tucking into a tasty ptarmigan.

Having hunted and killed a baby hare, this Arctic fox is about to eat him up.

Ferocious wolverines are capable of killing mammals much larger than they are. This one is feeding on a caribou carcass.

# To us, the Arctic seems a harsh and cruel place where food is scarce. Many animals survive by hunting, killing, and eating other creatures—a way of life that is common in nature. Animals that do this are known as predators.

Wolves cover huge distances across open icescapes in their search for food.

There's nothing a polar bear likes more than a delicious seal supper on sea ice.

# Acknowledgments

The publisher would like to thank the following for their kind permission to reproduce their photographs:

(Key: a-above; b-below/bottom; c-centre; f-far; l-left; r-right; t-top)

1 FLPA: Jurgen & Christine Sohns. 2 Getty Images: The Image Bank/Richard Ross (br). SeaPics.com: David B. Fleetham (bc). 2-3 Alamy Images: Steve Bloom Images (b). Still Pictures: L. C. Marigo (t). 3 Alamy Images: Blickwinkel/Hummel (ftr). Corbis: Anthony John West (bc). FLPA: Tui De Roy/Minden Pictures (tr); Michael & Patricia Fogden/Minden Pictures (tl). naturepl.com: Neil Lucas (br). 4 Alamy Images: Juniors Bildarchiv/F275 (ca). Ardea: Francois Gohier (bl). FLPA: Gerard Lacz (br). 5 Scubazoo.com: Jason Isley (br). Erwin & Peggy Bauer/Wildstock: (br). 6-7 Getty Images: Robert Harding World Imagery/Sergio Pitamitz. 8 Corbis: Stephen Fink (bl). Oceanwide Images: Gary Bell (tl). www.wildasia.net: Terence Lim (cr). 8-9 Oceanwide Images: Gary Bell. 9 Alamy Images: Fabrice Bettex (cr). Corbis: Stephen Fink (brr); Jeffrey L. Rotman (tl). Scubazoo.com: Jason Isley (cl). SeaPics.com: Gary Bell (tr). Alamy Images/Fredy J. Brauchli (r). 10 SeaPics.com: Peter Parks/iq-3d (tr, bl). 10-11 SeaPics.com: Randy Morse (l). Gary Bell (b); Peter Parks/iq-3d (c). 12 SeaPics.com: Robert Yin (t). Oceanwide Images: Gary Bell (b). 12-13 Oceanwide Images: Gary Bell. 13 Sue Scott: (b). SeaPics.com: Doug Perrine (tr). www.wildasia.net: Terence Lim (tl). 14 Chris Newbert/Minden Pictures (cla). SeaPics.com: David B. Fleetham; James D. Watt (b). Sub Aqua Images/Fredy J. Brauchli: (cla, br). 15 FLPA: Chris Newbert/Minden Pictures (t). Scubazoo.com: Jason Isley (br). SeaPics.com: James D. Watt (b). Sub Aqua Images/Fredy J. Brauchli: (clb, tr). 16 SeaPics.com: Doug Perrine (tl). Jon Bondy: (crb). Corbis: Tom Brakefield (tr). imagequestmarine.com: Roger Steene (tl); Scott Tuason (br). Photolibrary: Tobias Bernhard (tr). 18 SeaPics.com: Reinhard Dirscherl (r); Doug Perrine (tl). www.uw.no: Nils Aukan (bl). 18-19 SeaPics.com: Doug Perrine. 19 Corbis: Lawson Wood (tl). SeaPics.com: Doug Perrine (tr). 20 SeaPics.com: Reinhard Dirscherl (tr). www.uw.no: Nils Aukan (bl). 20-21 Oceanwide Images: Gary Bell (b). 21 Oceanwide Images: Gary Bell (tl, c). 22 SeaPics.com: Franco Banfi (tr); Doug Perrine (b). 22-23 SeaPics.com: Doug Perrine (c). 23 Oceanwide Images: Gary Bell (tl, cl, cla, tr). SeaPics.com: Doug Perrine (b). 24 SeaPics.com: Doug Perrine. 24-25 SeaPics.com: Doug Perrine. 25 Corbis: Bob Abraham (tl); Brandon D. Cole (cl). imagequestmarine.com: 2003 James D. Watt (br). Science Photo Library: Georgette Douwma (r). SeaPics.com: Doug Perrine (cra). Sub Aqua Images/Fredy J. Brauchli (cb). 26 SeaPics.com: Stephen Fink (bl); Stuart Westmorland (cr). 27 Corbis: Stuart Westmorland (r). SeaPics.com: David B. Fleetham (tl); Doug Perrine (cl). 28 Corbis: Darrell Gulin (c). NHPA/Photoshot: B. Jones & M. Shimlock (b). 28-29 FLPA: Norbert Wu/Minden Pictures. 29 Alamy Images: S.C. Bisserot/Worldwide Picture Library (crb). Corbis: Martin Harvey (br). FLPA: Shin Yoshino/Minden Pictures (t). Science Photo Library: Georgette Douwma (cra). SeaPics.com: Doug Perrine (tr). 30 Sub Aqua Images/Fredy J. Brauchli: (l). 30-31 Corbis: Lawson Wood (c). Sub Aqua Images/Fredy J. Brauchli: (b). 31 Corbis: Lawson Wood (tr). www.wildasia.net: Terence Lim (tr, cl). 32 Oceanwide Images: Gary Bell (bl). Norbert Wu: (tr). 32-33 Norbert Wu. 33 Jon Bondy: (crb). imagequestmarine.com: Roger Steene (cr). Photolibrary: (tl). Scubazoo.com: Jason Isley (cra, br, cl). 34 Sue Scott: (br). SeaPics.com: Doug Perrine (bl). 35 Corbis: Lawson Wood (tr). Sue Scott: (cl, br). www.wildasia.net: Terence Lim (cl). 36 Photolibrary: Dave Fleetham (bl). Scubazoo.com: Jason Isley. SeaPics.com: Mark Strickland (br). Treasure Images: Eric Madeja (tl). 37 Photolibrary: Dave Fleetham (cr). SeaPics.com: Mark Strickland (br); James D. Watt (cra). Treasure Images: Eric Madeja (tl). 38 SeaPics.com: Reinhard Dirscherl (br, t). 39 Corbis: Amos Nachoum (cr). Dr Frances Dipper: (clb). National Geographic Stock: David Doubilet (b). SeaPics.com: Shedd Aquar/Ceisel (cr). 40 Corbis: Lawson Wood (bl). FLPA: Norbert Wu/Minden Pictures (cr). Science Photo Library: Matthew Oldfield, Scubazoo (tl). 40-41 Science Photo Library: Matthew Oldfield, Scubazoo. 41 Alamy Images: Fabrice Bettex (cr). Ardea: Valerie Taylor (tr). Jon Bondy: (br). FLPA: Norbert Wu/Minden Pictures (bl). Scubazoo.com: Jason Isley (br). SeaPics.com: Doug Perrine (cra). 42 Corbis: Stephen Fink (b). 42-43 Alamy Images: James D Watt/Stephen Fink Collection. 43 Getty Images: Gary Bell (r); David Hall (r). 44 Corbis: Lawson Wood (bl). FLPA: Norbert Wu/Minden Pictures (tr). Norbert Wu: (tr). 45 Corbis: Jeffrey L. Rotman (bl); Douglas P. Wilson/Frank Lane Picture Agency (tl). FLPA: Norbert Wu/Minden Pictures (tr). naturepl.com: Georgette Douwma (r). 46 Science Photo Library: Alexis Rosenfeld (clb, bl). SeaPics.com: Doug Perrine (tl). 46-47 SeaPics.com: Doug Perrine. 47 Corbis: Kevin Schafer (tr). 48-49 NHPA/Photoshot: Martin Wendler. 50 Alamy Images: (tl). 50-51 Alamy Images. 51 Alamy Images: (cr). Ardea: (tl). FLPA: (tl). OSF: (r). stevebloom.com: (r). 52 Ardea: (tl). Corbis: Theo Allofs (bl). 53 Corbis: Kevin Schafer/Zefa. Still Pictures: (tr). 54 Alamy Images: (tl). Ardea: (tl). naturepl.com: (tl). 55 Alamy Images: (tl). Corbis: (tl). 56 Fauna & Flora International: (tl). FLPA: (tl, clb). NHPA/Photoshot: (cl). 57 Fauna & Flora International: (tl). FLPA: (tr, cra). OSF: (br). Photolibrary: Oxford Scientific. 58 Getty Images: Image Bank (tr). OSF: (bl, tl). Science Photo Library: (tr). 59 Corbis: (cl). FLPA: (cra). NHPA/Photoshot: (bl). Still Pictures: (br). 60 naturepl.com (br). 61 Corbis: Michael & Patricia Fogden (br). FLPA: (tr, cra, crb). 62 FLPA: (l, tr). Lonely Planet Images: (br). 63 Alamy Images: (tl); Brand X Pictures (br). NHPA/Photoshot: (tr). Still Pictures: (tr). 64 FLPA: (l, r). 65 FLPA: (br). FLPA: (tr). 66 NHPA/Photoshot: (tr). 67 FLPA: (tr, br, cr). OSF: (crb). Still Pictures: (cra). 68 Corbis: Michael & Patricia Fogden (br). FLPA: (r). Photolibrary: (br). 68-69 Photolibrary: (background). 69 Alamy Images: (r). Corbis: Michael & Patricia Fogden (r). FLPA: (cra, b, crb). 70 Arco Images: (r). Corbis: (tl); Arthur Morris (br). NHPA/Photoshot: (r). 71 Corbis: Michael & Patricia Fogden (tr). 72 FLPA: (br). Photolibrary: (br). 73 Corbis: Michael & Patricia Fogden (b). FLPA: (tr). Photolibrary: (br). 74 Corbis: Galen Rowell (tl). 75 Alamy Images: (r). Corbis: Tim Davis (tl). Das Fotoarchiv: (br). naturepl.com: (br). NHPA/Photoshot: (br). 76 Alamy Images: (tl). NHPA/Photoshot: (cla, bl, clb). Photolibrary: (br). 77 Corbis: Gary Braasch (background). FLPA: Photolibrary: (l). FLPA: (cla). naturepl.com: (clb, bl, r). Photolibrary: (br). 79 naturepl.com: (br). OSF: (tr, cra, bl). 80 naturepl.com: (br). OSF: (bl). 81 Ardea: (br). FLPA: (br). naturepl.com: (br). Photolibrary: (br). 82 FLPA: (b, tl). naturepl.com: (cb, tfl). NHPA/Photoshot: (tr, br, cr). 84 Photolibrary: (tr, br, cr). 85 FLPA: (r). Getty Images: National Geographic Stock: (r). Science Photo Library: (fbl, bl). 86 OSF: (t, bl). 87 NHPA/Photoshot: OSF: (c). Photolibrary: (tl, br). 89 FLPA: (br). Photolibrary: (r). 89 OSF: (r). Photolibrary: (br). 90-91 FLPA: David Hosking. 92 Alamy Images: Steve Bloom Images (b). 92-93 Alamy Images: Steve Bloom Images (b). 93 Ardea: Peter Steyn (tr). Corbis: Marcello Calandrini (cr); Martin Harvey (br); Martin Harvey; Gallo Images (tr). FLPA: Michael & Patricia Fogden/Minden Pictures (cra). 94 Alamy Images: Steve Bloom Images (l, cb). 94-95 Alamy Images: Steve Bloom Images (c). 95 Corbis: Tim Davis (cra); Mary Ann McDonald (c) and Paul A. Souders (br). 96-97 Getty Images: Daryl Balfour (c). 97 Alamy Images: Steve Bloom Images (br). Getty Images: Joanna Van Gruisen (br). Bruce Coleman Ltd: Carol Hughes (crb). Corbis: Tom Brakefield (tr). naturepl.com: Herman Brehm (b). 98 Alamy Images: Steve Bloom Images (bl). Corbis: Mary Ann McDonald (bl). 98-99 naturepl.com: Richard du Toit. 99 Ardea: Chris Harvey (br). Corbis: Lynda Richardson (cr); Ron Sanford (t). Getty Images: Jonathan & Angela Scott (br). 100 Wynand & Claudia Du Plessis: (tl). 100-101 Wynand & Claudia Du Plessis. 101 Alamy Images: Steve Bloom Images (br). Corbis: Roger Tidman (cr). Getty Images: Peter Lilja (t). naturepl.com: Terry Andrewartha (cr). 102 DK Images: Jerry Young (tl). Still Pictures: Heike Fischer (bl). 102-103 Photolibrary: Osolinski Stan (c). 103 Corbis: Gallo Images (tr); Clem Haagner; Gallo Images (crb). Still Pictures: Martin Harvey (cra). 104 Corbis: Gallo Images (tl); Wolfgang Kaehler (br). 105 Corbis: Rick Doyle (tl); Wolfgang Kaehler (br, bl). 106 Corbis: Nigel J. Dennis; Gallo Images (tl, br); Wolfgang Kaehler (cr). 107 Corbis: Steve Bein (tl); Gavin G. Thomson/Gallo Images (b); Winifred Wisniewski; Frank Lane Picture Agency (b). 108 Photolibrary: Michael Fogden (tl). 108-109 Photolibrary: Michael Fogden. 109 Corbis: Yann Arthus-Bertrand (tr); Martin Harvey (cr); William Manning (cra). FLPA: William S. Clark (r). Getty Images: Gallo Images/Heinrich van den Berg (br). 110 Corbis: Peter Johnson (cl). Getty Images: Gallo Images/Daryl Balfour (b). 110-111 Corbis: Roger De La Harpe/Gallo Images (c). 111 Corbis: Peter Johnson (tr). Getty Images: Darrell Gulin (t). 112 Alamy Images: David Wall (tl). Corbis: Joe McDonald (bl). 113 Corbis: Nigel J. Dennis/Gallo Images (tr). DK Images: Jerry Young (crb). naturepl.com: Richard du Toit (br). 114 Ardea: Clem Haagner (br). Corbis: Richard du Toit/Gallo Images (c). National Geographic Stock: Volkmar K. Wentzel (bl). 115 Alamy Images: Steve Bloom Images (tl). Ardea: Clem Haagner (bl). Corbis: Peter Johnson (br). naturepl.com: Sharon Heald (cra); Richard du Toit (crb). 116 National Geographic Stock: Chris Johns (l). 116-117 National Geographic Stock: Mattias Klum (bc). 117 National Geographic Stock: Mattias Klum (br). Roberta Stacey: (l). 118 Alamy Images: Steve Bloom Images (tl). Getty Images: Gallo Images/Heinrich van den Berg (bl). 118-119 Alamy Images: Steve Bloom Images (b). 119 Alamy Images: Steve Bloom Images (br). Getty Images: Darrell Gulin (cr). Getty Images: James Balog (tr). National Geographic Stock: Chris Johns (cra). Photolibrary: Alan Hartley (crb). 120 DK Images: Philip Dowell (tl). 120-121 National Geographic Stock: Chris Johns (b). 121 Bruce Coleman Ltd: Christer Fredriksson (r). naturepl.com: Richard du Toit (cl). 122 Corbis: Martin Harvey/Gallo Images (bl). 122-123 Corbis: Martin Harvey/Gallo Images (c). 123 Alamy Images: Martin Harvey (r). Corbis: Gallo Images (cla, cl, clb). Getty Images: Jonathan & Angela Scott (br). 124 NHPA/Photoshot: Jonathan & Angela Scott (l). 124-125 Corbis: Jeffrey L. Rotman (c). 125 Ardea: Clem Haagner (cr). National Geographic Stock: Kim Wolhuter (tl). naturepl.com: Sharon Heald (c); Ron O'Connor (crb). 126 Alamy Images: Steve Bloom Images (br, cl, cr). Corbis: Roger Tidman (crb). Getty Images: Roger Tidman (crb). Getty Images: Roger Tidman (cra). naturepl.com: Peter Blackwell (tr). 128 Corbis: Peter Johnson (tr); David A. Northcott (tr). National Geographic Stock: Kim Wolhuter (bl). 128-129 Corbis: David A. Northcott (c). 129 Corbis: Peter Johnson (br); George McCarthy (br). 130 Getty Images: Steve Bloom (tr). Bruce Coleman Ltd: John Shaw (b). 132-133 FLPA: Bob Gibbons. 134-135 Alain & Berny Sebe/www.alainsebeimages.com. 135 Ardea: Duncan Usher (b). FLPA: Yossi Eshbol (t); Chris Mattison (ca). Getty Images: National Geographic/Michael Melford (r); National Geographic/Carsten Peter (br). 136 FLPA: Mark Moffett/Minden (tr); Konrad Wothe/Minden (b). Alain & Berny Sebe/www.alainsebeimages.com: (c). 137 Ardea: Ken Lucas (tl). FLPA: David Hosking (b). NHPA/Photoshot: Martin Harvey (tr). 138 Alamy Images: David Hosking. 139 Alamy Images: Krys Bailey (crb). NHPA/Photoshot: Roland Seitre (t). 140 Getty Images: Digital Vision/Digital Zoo (tr). naturepl.com: Bernard Castelein (r). NHPA/Photoshot: Daniel Heuclin (r). 141 Eyal Bartov: (bl). FLPA: David Hosking (tl). Lonely Planet Images: Olivier Cirendini (cr). NHPA/Photoshot: Daniel Heuclin (br). 142-143 Alain & Berny Sebe/www.alainsebeimages.com. 143 Alamy Images: Blickwinkel (ca). Corbis: Craig Aurness (br). OSF: Waina Cheng (crb). Science Photo Library: George D. Lepp (cr). Still Pictures: Alain Dragesco-Joffe (cr). 144 Getty Images: Frans Lemmens (tl). NHPA/Photoshot: Daniel Heuclin (bl). 144-145 Natural Visions: Jason Venus (b). 145 Alamy Images: Gary Cook (tr). NHPA/Photoshot: Daniel Heuclin (tr, cra); Karl Switak (crb). 146 Corbis: Mitsuaki Iwago/Minden (br). naturepl.com: Anup Shah (br). 146-147 naturepl.com: Vincent Munier. 147 Mitsuaki Iwago/Minden (ca); Sunset (cb). naturepl.com: Karl Ammann (br). 148 Raymonde Bonnefille/sahara-nature.com (tl). 148 Gerry Ellis/Minden (br). 148-149 NHPA/Photoshot: Daniel Heuclin. 149 Raymonde Bonnefille/sahara-nature.com: (cr). 150-151 Alamy Images: Iconotec. 151 Alamy Images: Blickwinkel (ca). Corbis: (cr). Still Pictures: Alain Dragesco-Joffe (cr, crb); Frans Lemmens (br). 152-153 Corbis: Frans Lemmens. 153 fjexpeditions.com (t). Andras Zboray: (tr). 154 Corbis: Hans Schouten (tr). naturepl.com: Hanne & Jens Eriksen. NHPA/Photoshot: (cr). 154-155 FLPA: Konrad Wothe/Foto Natura. 155 FLPA: Duncan Usher (r). OSF: Manfred Pfefferle (r). Alain & Berny Sebe/www.alainsebeimages.com: (cr). Still Pictures: Alain Dragesco-Joffe (r). 157 Alamy Images: David J Slater (crb). Jan Beames (tr). naturepl.com: Hanne & Jens Eriksen (br); Neil Lucas (cra); Anup Shah (cr). 158 FLPA: Gerry Ellis/Minden (tr). 158-159 Imagestate: Philippe Saharoff/Explorer. 159 Alain & Berny Sebe/www.alainsebeimages.com: (cr). Still Pictures: Patricia Jordan (tr). 160 Still Pictures: Martin Harvey (tr). 160-161 Science Photo Library: Alan and Sandy Carey. 161 OSF: Alain Dragesco-Joffe (tl). Alain Dragesco-Joffe (tr). fjexpeditions-asso.org/Michel Aymerich: (tl). 162-163 fjexpeditions.com/Andras Zboray. 163 fjexpeditions.com/Andras Zboray: (tr, br, cr). NHPA/Photoshot: Chris Mattison (tl). 165 Getty Images: National Geographic/Carsten Peter (br). NHPA/Photoshot: Daniel Heuclin (cra); Christophe Ratier (crb). Robert Harding Picture Library: (cr). 166 FLPA: Yossi Eshbol (b). 166-167 Alain Dragesco-Joffe. 167 Alamy Images: David Hosking (br). alsirhan.com. OSF: Alain Dragesco-Joffe (bl). Still Pictures: Alain Dragesco-Joffe (br). 168 FLPA: David Hosking (bl). OSF: Eyal Bartov (c). 168-169 NHPA/Photoshot: Daniel Heuclin. 169 Alamy Images: Malie Rich-Griffith (tr). Still Pictures: Frans Lemmens (br). Erwin & Peggy Bauer/Wildstock: (tr). 170 NHPA/Photoshot: Daniel Heuclin (br). OSF: IFA-Bilderteam GmbH (br). 170-171 Alain & Berny Sebe/www.alainsebeimages.com. 171 www.geres-asso.org/Michel Aymerich: (cr, bl). NHPA/Photoshot: Daniel Heuclin (br). 172-173 Alamy Images: Craig Lovell/Eagle Visions Photography. 174 Alamy Images: Jan Baks (tl). 174-175 Alamy Images: Jan Baks. 175 FLPA: Tui De Roy/Minden Pictures (tr); Tim Fitzharris/Minden Pictures (b). naturepl.com: Jim Clare (ca); Gabriel Rojo (cb). Photolibrary: Mark Jones/Oxford Scientific (c). 176 Alamy Images: Les Gibbon (br). Ardea: François Gohier (r). FLPA: Tui De Roy/Minden Pictures (r). 176-177 Photolibrary: Oxford Scientific. 177 NHPA/Photoshot: Hans Christoph Kappel (tr); Pete Oxford (cr). NHPA/Photoshot: Otto Pfister (tl, b). 178 Alamy Images: Kevin Schafer (cr). naturepl.com: John Waters (tl). NHPA/Photoshot: Image Quest 3-D (l). 179 Alamy Images: Kevin Schafer (tl). naturepl.com: Gabriel Rojo (tl). 180 FLPA: Gabriel Rojo (tr). 180-181 FLPA: Tui De Roy. 181 Ardea: François Gohier (r). FLPA: Tui De Roy/Minden Pictures (cra, b). naturepl.com: Laurie Campbell (bl); Kevin Schafer (c). 182 FLPA: Yva Momatiuk/John Eastcott/Minden Pictures (tr); Jurgen & Christine Sohns (bl). naturepl.com: David Tipling (c). 182-183 naturepl.com: Daniel Gomez. 183 FLPA: John Hawkins (tl); Hans Hut/Foto Natura (bl); Frans Lanting/Minden Pictures (clb); R & M Van Nostrand (t); Tom Vezo/Minden Pictures (cr); Tony Wharton (tr). naturepl.com: Gabriel Rojo (bl). 184-185 Ardea: François Gohier. 185 Natural Science Photos: A. Mercieca (tl). 186 Corbis: Wolfgang Kaehler (tl). NHPA/Photoshot: Laurie Campbell (tr). 186-187 FLPA: Winifred Wisniewski. 187 FLPA: Tui De Roy/Minden Pictures (tl); Pete Oxford/Minden Pictures (tr). NHPA/Photoshot: Laurie Campbell (b); Jany Sauvanet (tr). 188 Corbis: Anthony John West (t). 188-189 Corbis: Anthony John West. 189 Alamy Images: Edward Parker (r). Laurie Campbell Photography: (c). FLPA: (t); Tui De Roy/Minden Pictures (cr). naturepl.com: Mike Potts (tr). 190 Andres Morya Photography: (br). Corbis: (l). naturepl.com: Pete Oxford (cra). 190-191 Getty Images: Posing Productions (b). 191 Getty Images: Robert Harding World Imagery (tl). naturepl.com:

Luiz Claudio Marigo (r). Professor Wayne A. Wurtsbaugh, Aquatic, Watershed & Earth Resources Dept./Ecology Center: (r). 192 FLPA: Tui De Roy/Minden Pictures (bl). naturepl.com: Hanne Jens Eriksen (cla). 192-193 naturepl.com: Rhonda Klevansky (t); Gabriel Rojo (b). 193 FLPA: Tui De Roy/Minden Pictures (cr). naturepl.com: Colin Seddon. NHPA/Photoshot: Lady Phillipa Scott (cr); Dave Watts (tc). 194 Corbis: Bob Rowan/Progressive Image (bl); Hubert Stadler (tr). 194-195 naturepl.com: Doug Allan. 195 Alamy Images: Homer Sykes (tr). Corbis: Hubert Stadler (tl). naturalimagebank.com/Mark Levesley: (br). naturepl.com: Doug Allan (tr). 196 Laurie Campbell Photography: (t). 196-197 Laurie Campbell Photography. 197 Corbis: Kevin Schafer (ca). FLPA: Tui De Roy/Minden Pictures (cb); Pete Oxford/Minden Pictures (c). NHPA/Photoshot: T Kitchin & V Hurst (r). 198 Evan Bowen-Jones/Fauna & Flora International: (r). National Geographic Stock: Joel Sartore (tl). 199 Alamy Images: Michele Falzone (cr); J Marshall - Tribaleye Images (b). National Geographic Stock: Joel Sartore (tl). Still Pictures: Juan Carlos Munoz (tr). 200 Getty Images: Purestock (b). Natural Science Photos: R Kemp (c). 201 Alamy Images: Terry Whittaker (tr). Corbis: Kevin Schafer (tl). NHPA/Photoshot: Jany Sauvanet (tr). FLPA: Jurgen & Christine Sohns (l). 202-203 Corbis: W. Perry Conway (b). 203 Laurie Campbell Photography: (cr). Getty Images: National Geographic (crb). NHPA/Photoshot: T Kitchin & V Hurst (r); John Shaw (tr). 204 FLPA: Tui De Roy/Minden Pictures (b). Paul Souders/WorldFoto. 204-205 Paul Souders/WorldFoto. 205 Alamy Images: Simon Littlejohn (b). Laurie Campbell Photography: (c). naturepl.com: Daniel Gomez (cb); Pete Oxford (t). Robert Harding Picture Library: Pete Oxford (r). 206 Alamy Images: Arco Images (l). FLPA: Pete Oxford (r). 207 Corbis: (t). FLPA: Mark Newman (crb). naturepl.com: Jim Clare (r). NHPA/Photoshot: Kevin Schafer (b); Dave Watts (t). 208 Alamy Images: Javier Etcheverry (r). FLPA: Hugh Clark (b). NHPA/Photoshot: Karl Switak (bl). 209 FLPA: Gerry Ellis/Minden Pictures (r); Chris Harvey (tr). FLPA: Tui De Roy/Minden Pictures (b). NHPA/Photoshot: T Kitchin & V Hurst (tr). 211 Alamy Images: Holger Ehlers (tr). FLPA: Foto Natura Stock (b). naturepl.com: Gabriel Rojo (br, cb); Colin Seddon (tl). 212-213 National Geographic Stock: R Lee Hopkins. 214 Corbis: Frank Lukasseck/Zefa. 214-215 Corbis: Frank Lukasseck/Zefa. 215 Alamy Images: Bryan And Cherry Alexander Photography (tr); Mark D (br). naturepl.com: Terry Andrewartha (cr); Steve Kazlowski (cr); Tom Mangelsen (crb). 216 Corbis: Tom Brakefield/Zefa (bl). 216-217 Corbis: Dan Guravich. 217 Corbis: Dan Guravich (b). Corbis: Alan & Sandy Carey/Zefa (bl). FLPA: Winifred Wisniewski/Foto Natura (tr). 218-219 Magnus Elander. 219 Ardea: M. Watson (tl). OSF: Norbert Rosing (r). 220 AlaskaStock.com: 2006 Steven Kazlowski. FLPA: Jim Brandenburgh/Minden Pictures. 221 Alamy Images: Image State (tr); Juniors Bildarchiv (r); Michio Hoshino/Minden Pictures (tr). 222 Alamy Images: John Schweider (cr). 222-223 Alamy Images: Steve Bloom Images. 223 Magnus Elander: (t, c, cl, cr). 224 Magnus Elander: (tl). 224 225 Magnus Elander. 225 Alamy Images: Bryan And Cherry Alexander Photography (tl); Steven J. Kazlowski (tr). Ardea: Dave White. Corbis: Theo Allofs (cr). naturepl.com: Niall Benvie (b); Asgeir Helgestad (cra). 226 Still Pictures: Kevin Schafer (tr). 226-227 Alamy Images: Bryan And Cherry Alexander Photography (c); Steven J. Kazlowski. 226 Alamy Images: blickwinkel (tr); Steven J. Kazlowski (br). Magnus Elander: (tl). 228 Alamy Images: David Fleetham (b). Corbis: Philip Jan Corwin (cr); Sea World of California (b). 229 Corbis: Douglas Wilson/FLPA (cl). FLPA: Flip Nicklin/Minden Pictures (r). OSF: Doug Allen (cl). 230 Alamy Images: Bryan And Cherry Alexander Photography. 230-231 Alamy Images: Bryan And Cherry Alexander Photography. 231 Alamy Images: Steven J. Kazlowski (tr). FLPA: Ron Austing (br); Jim Brandenburgh/Minden Pictures (br). Getty Images: Paul Hermansen (tr). Still Pictures: Kelvin Aitken (cr). 232 Alamy Images: D.Kjaer/TT National Trust Photo Library (tl). Bryan and Cherry Alexander Photography: FLPA: Flip de Nooyer/Foto Natura (cl); John Watkins (tr). 232-233 FLPA: David Hosking. 233 Corbis: Stuart Westmorland (tr). FLPA: Winifred Wisniewski (tr). Alamy Images: blickwinkel (t). Ardea: Andrey Zvoznikor (bl). 234-235 naturepl.com: Mike Potts. 235 Alamy Images: Arco Images (br); Visual & Written SL (tl, c). Corbis: Staffon Widstrand (bl). FLPA: Konrad Wothe/Minden Pictures (tr). naturepl.com: Tom Mangelsen (cr). 236 Alamy Images: Steven J. Kazlowski (cr). 236-237 Bryan and Cherry Alexander Photography: (r). 237 Alamy Images: Juniors Bildarchiv (tr); Steven J. Kazlowski (tr). Bryan and Cherry Alexander Photography: (cr). 238 Corbis: Hans Reinhard/Zefa (tr). 238-239 Corbis: Hans Reinhard/Zefa (b). Alamy Images: blickwinkel (tr). Corbis: John Swedberg (cr). naturepl.com: Andrey Zvoznikov (br). SuperStock: age foto stock (r). 240 OSF: Mark Hamblin (tl). 241 Alamy Images: Bryan And Cherry Alexander Photography (br); Marco Regalia (r). FLPA: Yva Momatiuk/John Eastcott/Minden Pictures (tl). 242 Alamy Images: Steven J. Kazlowski (tl, clb). Corbis: Tom Brakefield (cla). 242 243 FLPA: Jim Brandenburgh/Minden Pictures. 243 Corbis: Jacques Langevin/Sygma (t/background). Alamy Images: Jim Brandenburgh/Minden Pictures (tr, b); Yva Momatiuk/John Eastcott/Minden Pictures (bl). 244 Alamy Images: Arco Images (c). Magnus Elander (bl). 244-245 Bryan and Cherry Alexander Photography. 245 FLPA: Flip Nicklin/Minden Pictures (b). Magnus Elander: (tl). 246 Alamy Images: Steve Bloom Images. 246-247 Alamy Images: Steve Bloom Images. 247 Alamy Images: Steven Kazlowski (tr, crb). Corbis: George D. Lepp (tr). naturepl.com: Asgeir Helgestad (cra). Science Photo Library: E. R. Degginger (br). 248 Alamy Images: Steve Bloom Images (tr). 248-249 Alamy Images: Steven J. Kazlowski. 249 Alamy Images: Bryan And Cherry Alexander Photography (r, cr). Uwe Walz (cr). 250 naturepl.com: Mark Payne-Gill (cr). 250-251 FLPA: Rinie Van Muers/Foto Natura. 251 Bryan and Cherry Alexander Photography: (tl). naturepl.com: Asgeir Helgestad (r). 252-253 Corbis: Frank Lukasseck. 254-255 naturepl.com: Daniel Gomez. 256 FLPA: Frans Lanting/Minden Pictures.

All other images © Dorling Kindersley
For further information see: www.dkimages.com

**Dorling Kindersley would like to thank:**

Rob Nunn for picture research, and Wendy Horobin and Penny Smith for proofreading.